Dangerous Creatures

of the
Tropical Rain Forests

Helen Bateman and Jayne Denshire

Smart Apple Media

This edition first published in 2005 in the United States of America by Smart Apple Media.

Smart Apple Media
1980 Lookout Drive
North Mankato
Minnesota 56003

First published in 2005 by
MACMILLAN EDUCATION AUSTRALIA PTY LTD
627 Chapel Street, South Yarra 3141

Visit our website at www.macmillan.com.au

Associated companies and representatives throughout the world.

Library of Congress Cataloging-in-Publication Data

Bateman, Helen.
  Of the tropical rainforests / by Helen Bateman and Jayne Denshire.
  p. cm. – (Dangerous creatures)
  Includes index.

  ISBN 1-58340-769-3

  1. Rain forest animals—Juvenile literature. 2. Dangerous animals—Tropics—Juvenile literature. I. Denshire, Jayne. II. Title.
  QL112.B362 2005
  691.734—dc22

                                                        2005042861

Project management by Limelight Press Pty Ltd
Design by Stan Lamond, Lamond Art & Design
Illustrations by Edwina Riddell
Maps by Laurie Whiddon, Map Illustrations. Adapted by Lamond Art & Design
Research by Kate McAllan

Consultant: George McKay PhD, Conservation Biologist

Printed in China

Acknowledgments
The authors and the publisher are grateful to the following for permission to reproduce copyright material:

Cover photograph: saltwater crocodile feeding on large fish, courtesy of Michael Cermak, ANTphoto.com.

Martin Harvey/ANTPhoto.com pp. 20, 26; Clive Bormhall-OSF/AUSCAPE p. 23; John Brown-OSF/AUSCAPE p. 14; Tui De Roy/AUSCAPE p. 29; Ferrero-Labat/AUSCAPE p. 22; Francois Gohier/AUSCAPE p. 19 (top); Luiz Marigo-Peter Arnold/AUSCAPE p. 9; Joe McDonald/AUSCAPE p. 21 (top); Patricio Robles Gill/AUSCAPE p. 8 (left); John Sauvanet/AUSCAPE p. 17; APL/Corbis/Tom Brakefield pp. 10, 13, 18–19; APL/Corbis/Patricia Fogden p. 11 (top); APL/Corbis/Martin Harvey pp. 7, 15; APL/Corbis/Gary Lewis p. 25; APL/Corbis/W. Perry Conway p. 11 (bottom); APL/Corbis/Kevin Schafer pp. 27, 29; APL/Corbis/Staffan Widstrand p. 8 (right); GettyImages/Stuart Westmorland p. 16; GettyImages/National Geographic/Mattias Klum p. 21 (bottom); Hans & Judy Beste Lochman Transparencies p. 24; Brett Dennis Lochman Transparencies p. 5; Digital Stock p. 6; Corbis p. 7; Digital Vision Ltd p. 12–13.

Please note
At the time of printing, the Internet addresses appearing in this book were correct. Owing to the dynamic nature of the Internet, however, we cannot guarantee that all these addresses will remain correct.

Contents

When a word is printed in **bold**, you can look up its meaning in the Glossary on page 31.

Life in the tropical rain forests

Tropical rain forests are areas of thick forest that grow in wet, tropical parts of the world. They cover only six percent of the Earth's surface, yet are home to more than half of all plants and animals.

Different types of vegetation grow in different levels of the rain forest, depending on how much light the plants need and get, and how much moisture gets to the plants. The tropical rain forest is home to many animals, some that live on the ground and others high in the trees.

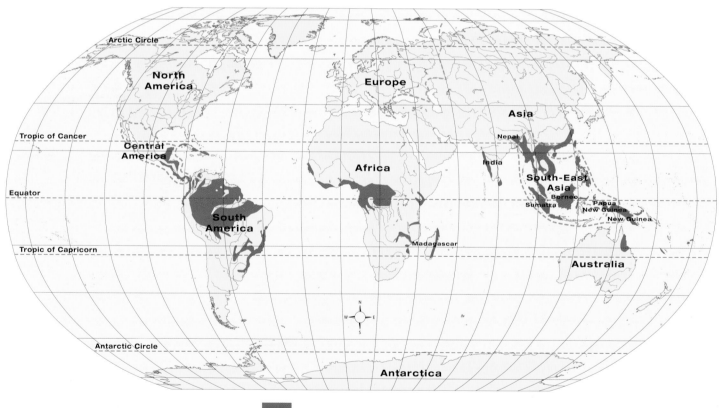

Tropical rain forests of the world

▲ There are two types of rain forest: temperate and tropical. Tropical rain forests grow close to the equator where lots of rain falls and it is always warm. Just outside the tropical zones are the slightly cooler subtropical rain forests.

► Half of the world's animals live in the trees, on the ground, or in the waters of tropical rain forests.

Level 4

harpy eagle

Level 3

tree snake

Level 2

caterpillar

Level 1   tall trees

▲ This is a food chain for the emergent level of the rain forest. Each animal in this chain feeds off the animal below it.

Danger and survival

Animals behave dangerously because they need to survive in their **habitat**. All creatures have to find food and shelter and often need to defend themselves against other animals at the same time. For many creatures, it is a case of kill or be killed.

Life in tropical rain forests is not always safe. These hot, wet places are full of danger—in the trees, in the water, and on the ground. At each level of rain forest growth, creatures need to be on the lookout for **predators**. Small animals on the ground are often an easy target for bigger animals in search of food. Some creatures may look harmless, but have hidden weapons which they use to survive.

Like all habitats, rain forest life is connected by **food chains**. Different food chains exist in the different growth layers—on the **forest floor**, in the **canopy**, and in the high **emergent** level. Living things at each level relate to each other in some way, either as food, or as predator. So animals at one level of the chain can be a threat or be threatened by the other animals at another level.

5

Bengal tigers

VITAL STATISTICS

LENGTH
up to ten feet (3.1 m) (including tail)

WEIGHT
up to 661 pounds (300 kg)

WHERE FOUND
India, Nepal

Bengal tigers are the largest of the big cats and one of the most powerful. As fierce predators, they wander through the grasses and bushes of the forest floor in search of fleshy creatures that will satisfy their hunger. They will also attack humans if other **prey** is scarce, or if humans go into their territory. This dangerous behavior towards humans is not common, but there have been reports of tigers attacking and viciously killing hunters and fishermen in rain forest areas.

Hidden stalkers

The colors and texture of tigers' coats provide excellent **camouflage** when stalking their prey. Their stripes blend with the surrounding grasses, making it hard for victims to spot these clever prowlers, especially at dusk when the light is less bright. Tigers have a very powerful head with strong bones that help them to bite with a killing blow. Their soft and sensitive paws allow them to move silently, in search of their prey.

◄ The Bengal tiger's senses are very alert, so it can locate a victim far away. Once the tiger spots its prey, it will often attack from behind.

In for the kill

Once a tiger grabs its prey in its teeth and claws, it brings the animal to the ground and suffocates it by breaking its neck or crushing its windpipe. The tiger then drags its kill under a bush so it can eat without being interrupted. Once it has had its fill, the tiger covers the **carcass** with leaves, ready for a later feed.

▲ A tiger's teeth are designed for tearing through flesh. Its long, front teeth are used for stabbing into the victim. Its side teeth slice through the meat.

▲ Male tigers will fight to protect their territory or to win a female. They often make coughing sounds when they attack each other.

fact flash

Tigers like water and are good swimmers. They often carry their dead prey across water, sometimes for many miles. They go into water backward, so they can keep watch around them.

Jaguars

fact flash

Jaguars that live in forests are darker than other jaguars. Sometimes they are almost all black.

VITAL STATISTICS

LENGTH
up to nine feet (2.65 m) (including tail)

WEIGHT
up to 353 pounds (160 kg)

WHERE FOUND
northern South America, Central America

Jaguars are smaller than many of the other big cats, especially the ones that live in rain forests, but they are very powerful and dangerous. They spend much of their time near rivers and water sources, in search of prey that comes to the water to drink or swim. These secretive creatures are only a danger to humans when people come too close to their territory, or when there is not enough of their usual food.

Jaguars mostly live and hunt alone, only joining other jaguars when they are ready to mate. They find their prey during the early evening when the light is low and it is hard to see. Sometimes jaguars will swim across wide rivers in an effort to capture their prey.

▼ Jaguars often perch in a tree to spot their prey, especially in the wet season when the forest floor is flooded.

▲ A jaguar uses its side teeth to cut the meat. Its sharp front teeth are shorter and wider than those of other big cats, yet it has the most powerful bite of all.

Forest hideaway

One of the best weapons jaguars have is their sandy coat with black blotches, which helps them to stay hidden from their prey. Their legs are shorter and stockier than those of other cats because jaguars are usually tree climbers. Their long, curved claws help them to move along branches and drag their victim to the ground.

Favorite food

On the ground, jaguars hunt capybaras (large south American **rodents**) and in the trees they attack sloths or other tree-dwellers. Near water, turtles and tortoises are often the target. After the jaguar has grabbed its victim, it crushes the skull with its strong teeth and jaws.

▼ Like other big cats, jaguars mark out their territory and will fight off other jaguars for the right to keep it.

9

Crocodilians

Crocodilians are a group of reptiles that are the largest and most dangerous in the world. They can hide almost completely underwater because their eyes and nostrils are high on their heads. They swallow their prey whole.

VITAL STATISTICS
LENGTH
up to 23 feet (7 m)
WEIGHT
up to one ton (1 t)
WHERE FOUND
northern Australia,
Southeast Asia

Saltwater crocodiles

These dangerous reptiles are the only crocodilians to live in salt water. They are found in tropical regions and swim in the ocean as well as up freshwater streams for many miles.

Big appetites

These crocodiles live off large **mammals** such as pigs, wallabies, cattle, and sometimes, humans. They will **scavenge** from dead animals but prefer freshly killed meat. When hunting prey, crocodiles keep their body hidden underwater with just their eyes and nostrils showing. Once they spot a victim on land, they dive underwater, then attack, snapping their jaws so tightly around them that there is no escape. Crocodiles then often drag their victim into water and drown it, ready for eating.

▲ The crocodile's teeth are replaced throughout its life so they stay sharp and strong for sinking into flesh.

▼ The snout of the crocodile is narrower than the caiman's. The crocodile's lower fourth tooth sits outside its bite when it closes its mouth.

lower fourth tooth

black caiman side view

American crocodile side view

black caiman top view

American crocodile top view

Black caimans

Like crocodiles, these reptile giants are a danger to rain forest mammals and fish, which fall victim to their strong jaws and deadly bite.

Water detectives

In the wet season, black caimans search the waters of the Amazon and the flooded rain forests for prey. They have such strong jaws that they can grab hold of large animals, such as buffalo or pigs, and tear them apart. These huge predators are able to tip boats over with one knock, but have rarely killed humans.

Sometimes when parents leave young caimans alone, jaguars and other predators will eat them if they get the chance.

▲ Black caimans often eat fish during the dry season because the fish all gather in smaller pools and cannot escape the caimans' bite.

◄ Like most other crocodilians, black caimans like to lie on hard, dry ground and soak up the sun. Their dark color acts as a disguise for unsuspecting prey nearby.

11

Poison-dart frogs

VITAL STATISTICS

LENGTH
0.5 to 2.5 inches
(1.2–6 cm)

WEIGHT
up to 18 ounces
(500 g)

WHERE FOUND
northern South
America

These brilliantly colored frogs may look pretty but they are one of the most dangerous creatures in the rain forest. They live inside plants called bromeliads, which are commonly found growing on rain forest trees. Although these miniature hunters eat insects as their prey, their deadliest weapon comes from their skin, which produces poison. The poison is used in darts by human hunters to kill other animals.

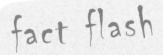

fact flash

Female poison-dart frogs can lay special unfertilized eggs to feed their young.

► Poison-dart frogs live both on the forest floor and in the trees. They mate in pairs away from the water.

▲ Many poison-dart frogs live inside bromeliads. The black and yellow stripes of this variety act as a warning sign for other creatures to stay away.

Delicate but deadly

Like most frogs, poison-dart frogs have a soft body that can be easily hurt. They need to keep themselves moist to stop their delicate skin from drying out. Their poison is **secreted** through **glands** in the skin, and as the frogs grow older, the poison becomes more deadly.

The variety of colors seen among poison-dart frogs is endless, ranging from brilliant blues and greens to bright yellows and reds.

Poison potion

A poison-dart frog's poison is often spread when a predator attacks the frog without realizing it is poisonous. Even if the frog is not swallowed, a tiny bit of the poison on the skin or mouth can be very painful and can cause severe illness. If the frog is swallowed, the poison can cause a heart attack within moments.

Hunters in the rain forests of South America dip darts into the frog's poison, then blow the dart at animals they want to kill. The dart enters the victim's body, paralyzing it, so that the hunter can pick up the still creature.

DANGER REPORT

Scientists in Colombo, South America, are now wondering whether the strength of the golden poison frog's poison—one of the most deadly species of poison-dart frogs—is caused by one of the small insects these frogs eat. The scientists think that perhaps this insect contains the poison that gets passed onto the frog when it eats the insect.

Army ants

VITAL STATISTICS

LENGTH
up to 0.5 inch
(1.2 cm)

WHERE FOUND
South America,
central Africa

Army ants are among the tiniest creatures in rain forests, and the most terrifying. They travel in huge numbers in search of their prey and are a danger to even the largest creatures. These ants do not have a permanent home. Instead they move around, constantly in search of their next victim. When they arrive at a new camp, they make their homes under stones or logs, or in the hollows of trees.

fact flash

Worker ants and soldier ants never breed. Special ants are bred for that. Worker ants collect food and look after the young ants. Soldier ants defend the colony. The queen ant produces offspring then dies once she breeds.

On the move

Army ants march in line formations with different ants in the colony, or community, taking up different positions. The worker ants cannot see, so they travel beside the soldier ants who can see and show them the way. In the center of the traveling "army" is the queen ant and the younger developing ants. The only thing that stops the ants in their tracks is fire, and humans will use this to fight off the ants if they are being attacked.

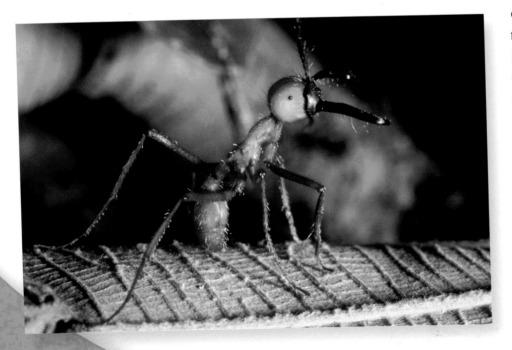

◄ When an army ant is ready to attack, it takes on a special pose, high on its legs. It then attacks, trying to satisfy its hunger for meat.

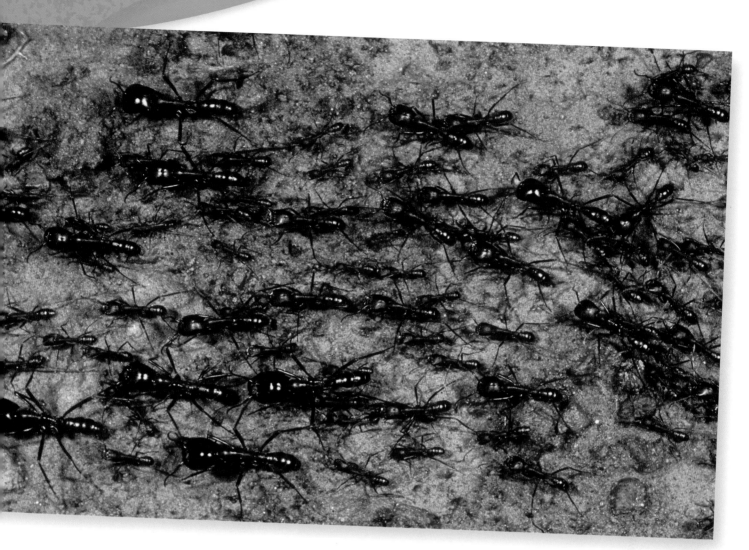

Search and destroy

Army ants do not just eat insects. They attack almost any animal that does not get out of their way quickly enough. Once they set up camp, the soldier and worker ants go out in search of prey. They stir up the leaf litter as they scramble all over the ground. Once they have found their victim they swarm over it in huge numbers and tear it apart.

These ants have been known to kill crocodiles, lizards, and rats, and have driven elephants mad.

▲ Army ants travel in columns that are several ants across. With so many ants marching at a time, they take many hours to get past one spot.

fact flash

When army ants cross water, some of the ants form a bridge with their bodies for the other ants to cross over. Some of the ants in the bridge will die, giving up their own life for the good of the colony.

15

Red-bellied piranhas

VITAL STATISTICS

LENGTH
up to 13 inches
(33 cm)

WEIGHT
up to 2 pounds (1 kg)

WHERE FOUND
South America

Not all piranhas are dangerous, but red-bellied piranhas certainly are. This species of piranha are meat-eaters and they can devour animals as large as a horse in minutes with their vicious, aggressive behavior. They are most dangerous during the rain forest dry season when there is not much water in rivers and the current is still. These fish are also vicious while they are breeding. Once the adults lay eggs, they guard them fiercely until they hatch. They will attack any creature that comes too close.

A warning color

Red-bellied piranhas are brilliant red on their head and belly. Tiny scales cover their body with thicker scales on their head to protect it when they headbutt a dead animal during feeding. Their protruding jaws help them to feed fast and furiously. They find their prey by using their sense of smell. They usually hunt and feed at either end of the day. This is the time they pose the greatest threat.

◄ Red-bellied piranhas often travel in shoals in search of their prey. They hunt for larger victims, which they can frantically attack as a group, in the same way sharks do.

Blood magnet

Red-bellied piranhas are attracted to blood and will often choose a wounded animal as their victim because they can sense where it is in the water from its trail of blood. They use their set of razor-sharp teeth as a trap, which clamps around the victim, then tears the flesh away from the animal's bones.

These piranhas have been known to attack humans, especially when the fish go after them in groups called shoals.

▲ The interlocking, triangular teeth and strong jaw of the red-bellied piranha can strip the flesh off an animal's bones in a few minutes.

Rain forest snakes

Many varieties of snake live in the rain forest. They include big tree-dwellers and huge swimmers. Most of the rain forest snakes use their colorings to blend with the surrounding habitat.

VITAL STATISTICS

LENGTH
up to 33 feet (10 m)

WEIGHT
up to 551 pounds
(250 kg)

WHERE FOUND
South America

Green anacondas

These massive snakes are heavy as well as long. They are one of the most dangerous rain forest creatures because they can **suffocate** their victim with great ease. Humans are not safe from green anacondas as these snakes are able to **strangulate** then eat them, as long as they fit into their mouth.

Power to swallow

Anacondas are excellent swallowers. Their jaws are only loosely connected to their skull, which allows the jaws to move more easily, and their throat is very stretchy. Their teeth point toward the back of their throat to make it easier for them to swallow and to help them grip their meal. They have no breastbone, so that once their food gets past their mouth it can be easily swallowed. Their eyes, which they cannot close, and nostrils are on the top of their head.

fact flash

Anacondas hear through their skull bones and they smell through their tongue.

DANGER REPORT

In 1999, a field assistant implanted a radio transmitter into a green anaconda's mouth to study an infection it had. When she tried to read the transmitter, the anaconda leapt at her and went for her knee but it only got hold of her pants. The snake struck again, but could not get a firm grip so the assistant was able to escape.

Squeeze of death

Anacondas kill their prey by **constriction**. Once they have their victim in their grip, they gradually tighten their hold each time the animal breathes out until it cannot breathe any more. This also stops the blood flow, which causes death. Anacondas often swim in shallow water near riverbanks, waiting to grab prey that comes to the edge to drink.

Animals such as young jaguars, capybaras, and deer are all at risk when an anaconda is close by. Large water creatures, such as turtles and caimans, can also be attacked.

▲ An anaconda grabs hold of its victim in its coils, then squeezes the animal's chest bit by bit until it can no longer breathe.

◄ Anacondas are strong swimmers. Their green and brown blotchy skin makes them hard to see under muddy water.

VITAL STATISTICS

LENGTH
up to eight feet
(2.4 m)

WHERE FOUND
New Guinea,
northern Australia

▼ Green tree
pythons will coil
themselves around
a tree branch and
point their head
down, waiting to
ambush their prey.
They also catch
water in their coils,
which they drink.

Green tree pythons

The bright green skin of these dangerous snakes that live in the rain forest canopy looks attractive, but is really a cover for deadly behavior. It also acts as a **camouflage** against birds of prey.

Swallowed whole

Green tree pythons first strangle their victim by wrapping their coils tightly around the victim's body. Then they swallow it whole, which usually takes time. Animals, such as small mammals and birds, gradually disappear down the python's throat as this gulping reptile uses its teeth to move the victim farther and farther back into its mouth. It repeats the action, first using the teeth on one side, then the other. It sometimes waves its blue tail tip in the air, possibly as a **lure** for its prey.

fact flash
Young green tree pythons are red or yellow, then turn green as they mature.

King cobras

King cobras are the longest **venomous** snakes in the world. Because they are so big, they are able to kill most other snakes with their venom. King cobras live on the rain forest floor. They are more dangerous in the breeding season when the females defend their nests until their babies hatch.

Standover tactics

When king cobras attack other snakes, they rear up over the snake and strike downward. They lift their long ribs up and away from their body to make themselves look bigger and more threatening to their victim. They aim their bite just behind the head of their prey so that the other snake cannot twist around and bite them back. The king cobra's venom can kill a human within minutes, although it is shy and tends to escape rather than attack.

▲ When a king cobra is threatened, it raises a third of its body off the ground and flares its hood, which is made up of the flaps of skin either side of its upper body.

fact flash

Indian cobras are related to king cobras. They do not hear the music that snake charmers play, but their eyes follow the music pipe's movement, which makes the snake sway.

► King cobras will often eat other king cobras, swallowing them headfirst. When they are eaten like this, the venom is not poisonous to other king cobras.

Chimpanzees

▼ Males will come face to face with each other when they are fighting for territory or for a female, showing their teeth as a sign of aggression.

Large groups of male and female chimpanzees live together in the rain forest. The males are the most dangerous, especially when they are defending their territory or fighting for the right to mate with the females in the group. The rain forest environment is ideally suited to these creatures, who spend much of their time high in the trees where they are safe from predators. They eat mostly forest fruits and insects, and the male chimpanzees hunt larger animals.

fact flash

Chimpanzees spend a lot of time grooming each other as a sign of affection, often when they want to make up after a fight.

Body weapons

Chimpanzees use their teeth and strength as their main weapons in attack. They have strong hands and feet, which help them to climb trees and move along quickly. On their hands is an **opposable** thumb, which allows them to pick up small nuts, berries, and sticks. Chimpanzees' arms are more flexible than their legs and hang below their knees. Their spine is not as strong as a human spine and their leg muscles are not as developed, so that they cannot stand upright for long periods.

Hungry chimpanzees will poke sticks into termite or fire ant nests, trying to find a meal. They risk being bitten when they try to swallow their catch.

Fighting the enemy

Male chimpanzees protect their own territory and sometimes make raids on others to claim as their own. They will fight for territory, beating and kicking each other. If a new male takes over, he may try to kill the babies of the last head male so that he can mate with the mother and have his own offspring. During these battles, males will kill other males and steal away the females.

In the **dry season** when there is not much fruit around, males will hunt larger animals such as antelopes or baboons. Chimpanzees often hunt together, blocking the escape paths for their victims. Once they catch their prey, they beat their prey on the ground or against branches. They are so strong that they can pull the dead animal apart with their hands.

▶ Chimpanzees often screech or scream during battle. The males have large canine teeth, which they use in vicious fights and to kill their prey.

Whistling spiders

VITAL STATISTICS

LENGTH
up to two inches
(5.5 cm)

WHERE FOUND
northern Australia,
Papua New Guinea

Whistling spiders are dangerous to other creatures who try to attack them. When the spiders are attacked they do not run away but instead fight back. These large, hairy hunters live in the rain forest, in burrows under rocks or in logs. They use their burrows to catch prey during the day then leave the burrows at night to find food on the floor of the forest.

Also known as barking spiders, they get their name from the noise they make when they are threatened, which sounds a bit like a bark or a whistle. To make this sound, they rub tiny hairs together very quickly, just near their mouth.

fact flash

The male spider dies soon after it mates but females can live for up to 10 years.

▼ The whistling spider's fangs are fixed to its body in fang bases. These are solid and strong and help the spider to crush its prey.

Big, hairy, and scary

Whistling spiders are among some of the biggest spiders in Australia. They belong to a genus, or group, called *Selenocosmia*. Like all spiders, these spiders have a number of eyes. Two eyes see objects and the others sense movement. Their legs are covered with sensitive hairs, which allow them to detect when they have caught prey.

fact flash

Whistling spiders have a long life, often living for more than 25 years.

Powerful weapons

Large **fangs** and strong venom mean that a whistling spider can kill quite large prey, including frogs, insects, lizards, and even birds. In less than six hours, a whistling spider is able to kill and eat a tree frog. Once it has stunned its victim with the venom, the spider uses its saliva to turn its prey into mush, ready for eating. Although the venom can kill animals, humans cannot die from a bite.

▲ **Whistling spiders make long, winding burrows under rocks or in logs. They spin a silky web across the front of the burrow, which acts as a trap for prey.**

Southern cassowaries

VITAL STATISTICS

HEIGHT
up to six feet (1.7 m)

WEIGHT
up to 154 pounds
(70 kg)

WHERE FOUND
northeastern
Australia,
Papua New Guinea

These heavy, flightless birds do not usually attack without a reason, but they can behave dangerously if they are cornered or hurt. When humans get in their way or make them angry, cassowaries see them as their enemy. Normally, these birds roam through rain forests looking for fruit. They do eat meat, usually in the form of insects and snails, but tend to live on leaves, fruits, and **fungi** as part of their everyday diet. The large bone on top of their heads is called a casque.

▲ When cassowaries are young, they are covered in soft feathers which are not stiff. As they get older, their feathers stiffen, their colors develop, and their casque grows.

▶ Cassowaries are brightly colored around their head and neck. They use their casque to ram their way through dense forest.

Foot dagger

The inner toes on the southern cassowary's huge feet are its greatest weapon. Each foot has three toes and the inner toe has a long, sharp claw. Cassowaries will use these claws to inflict wounds on their victim. These birds have stiff feathers around their shoulders, which can also cause injuries. The females weigh more and stand taller than the males.

Claiming their territory

Southern cassowaries mostly live alone in their own territory. Sometimes when two birds meet in a territory, they will fight to claim the area, and to drive the other bird away. If a cassowary feels threatened by a human, it will hiss and stamp its feet, and make a drumming noise as a warning to stay away. If the human does not move, the cassowary will kick with its feet high in the air so that the toe claws cut into the victim's flesh.

DANGER REPORT

In 1926 in Queensland, Australia, two brothers went with their hunting dog to look for two lost horses in the local bush. While there, their dog was attacked by a huge cassowary. When one brother tried to rescue the dog the cassowary leapt at him and kicked him in the throat, causing a huge gash in his main neck vein. He later died.

Harpy eagles

VITAL STATISTICS

WINGSPAN
up to seven feet (2 m)

WEIGHT
up to 20 pounds (9 kg)

WHERE FOUND
Central America,
northern South America

These birds of prey are the largest and most powerful **raptors** in the world, and they pose great danger for many creatures that live on the ground of the rain forest. Harpy eagles perch themselves high in the branches of rain forest trees, trawling the ground for prey with their keen eyes. They are excellent fliers and will soar from great heights to catch their prey. Sometimes, they sit in wait near rivers or clearings for creatures that come to drink or to graze.

Predator on high

Harpy eagles have short wings in comparison to their size, so they can fly safely between trees without hurting themselves, and can move swiftly toward their target. They have a pale face with darker markings near their black beak, and brown and white body feathers that ruffle as part of their aggressive behavior. Their powerful feet enable them to grasp tightly onto their victim. They then sink their front claws and larger, dagger-like rear **talon** into the victim's flesh.

◀ As a typical member of the raptor group, the harpy eagle has excellent eyesight, a hooked beak, and sharp, strong talons.

▼ When harpy eagles are threatened or hungry, they fluff up their neck and head feathers, and raise their crest of feathers, ready for attack.

fact flash

The talons of a harpy eagle are three times stronger than the jaws of a Rottweiler dog and can crush a human's arm in a single action.

fact flash

If human eyes were as big as a harpy eagle's eyes compared to their head size, the human eyes would each weigh a few pounds.

Monkey business

Harpy eagles hunt many different rain forest animals but they are the greatest threat to monkeys and to sloths. Once the eagles spot their next victim, they soar down and grab it with their razor-sharp talons. The talons need to be strong enough to hang on to such heavy prey. The victim can die from the eagle's first strike but if not, the eagle stabs its sharp back talon into the flesh like a knife.

Endangered animals
of the
tropical rain forests

More than 5,000 animal species in the world today are endangered. They are in danger from their competitors and predators, and they are in danger from natural disasters, such as droughts, floods, and fires.

But the greatest threat to animals comes from the most dangerous animals of all—humans. As more and more people fill the Earth, there is less room for wildlife. Humans clear land to put up buildings. They farm land for crops or grazing, or they mine it to produce fuel. Precious wildlife habitats are destroyed.

Here are just some of the animals that are in danger of vanishing forever from the tropical rain forests of this planet.

ENDANGERED ANIMAL	WHERE FOUND
Chimpanzee	Central west Africa
Harpy eagle	Central America, Northern South America
Lion-tailed macaque	India
Mandrill	West Africa
Mongoose lemur	Madagascar
Mountain gorilla	Central Africa
Orangutan	Borneo and Sumatra
Saltwater crocodile	Northern Australia, Southeast Asia
Southern cassowary	Northeastern Australia, Papua New Guinea
Tiger	Asia

You can find out more about saving the world's wildlife by visiting the World Wildlife Fund (WWF) at http://www.panda.org.

Glossary

camouflage something in an animal's appearance that helps it to blend into the background

canopy the main layer of the rainforest where tree tops grow to between 65 and 164 feet above the ground

carcass the dead body of an animal

constriction the method snakes use to crush their prey by tightening their coils around the victim

dry season a dry, cooler period of time in a tropical area when not much rain falls

emergent the top layer of the rain forest with the tallest trees. They extend above 164 feet (50 m)

fangs long, sharp, hollow teeth that are used by snakes to inject venom

food chains the relationships between living things. They show which animals eat which in order to survive

forest floor the part of the rain forest with the least light where mosses and ferns grow, and leaves and branches litter the ground. The largest animals live there

fungi simple plants, such as mushrooms, that grow in damp or dark places

glands body parts that produce a substance used somewhere else in the body

habitat an animal's natural living place

lure something that attracts

mammals animals whose young feed on their mother's milk

opposable describes a finger or toe that is able to touch the soft tips of the other fingers or toes

predators animals that hunt and kill other animals

prey animals that are caught and eaten by other animals

raptors one of the main group of birds of prey, with hooked beaks, strong feet, sharp talons, and large eyes

rodents the group of gnawing or nibbling mammals, such as rats and mice

scavenge to feed off dead animals

secreted when a substance, such as poison, is separated from the blood in the glands

strangulate to kill by stopping the flow of air, by constriction

suffocate to kill by stopping air flow to the lungs, which in turn stops breathing

talon a claw, especially for grasping or for attacking

venomous poisonous

Index